Roy Keane

In the bustling town of Cork, Ireland, on a warm August day in 1971, Roy Maurice Keane came into the world, a bundle of energy destined to make his mark on the footballing world.

From his earliest days kicking a ball around the local fields, it was evident that Keane possessed a rare talent and an unyielding determination. His journey to greatness began with humble roots, playing for Cobh Ramblers before catching the eye of scouts and making his mark in the professional leagues.

But it was at Nottingham Forest and later Manchester United where Keane truly shone. With his commanding presence in midfield and a ferocious competitive spirit, he became a cornerstone of Sir Alex Ferguson's legendary Manchester United squad. Under his leadership as captain, the team soared to unprecedented heights, claiming seven Premier League titles, four FA Cups, and the prestigious UEFA Champions League.

Keane's reputation as one of the finest midfielders of his generation was cemented when he found himself named among the FIFA 100, an illustrious list of the greatest living footballers, handpicked by none other than the legendary Pelé himself.
Yet, Keane's journey wasn't without its tumultuous moments. His unwavering passion occasionally boiled over, leading to infamous clashes both on and off the pitch. One such incident saw him sent home from the 2002 FIFA World Cup after a heated dispute with the national team's coach, Mick McCarthy.

Following his illustrious playing career, Keane transitioned into management, showcasing his leadership skills once more. At Sunderland, he engineered a remarkable turnaround, guiding the team from the depths of the Football League Championship to Premier League promotion.

His managerial journey took him to various clubs, including a stint at Ipswich Town, where he continued to leave an indelible mark on the footballing landscape. Keane's influence extended beyond the touchline, as he lent his expertise as a studio analyst for renowned football broadcasts.

In 2021, the Premier League recognized Keane's enduring legacy by inducting him into the prestigious Hall of Fame, a testament to his unparalleled contributions to the beautiful game.

Through triumphs and trials, Roy Keane's story is one of passion, perseverance, and an unwavering commitment to excellence—a story that will echo through the annals of football history for generations to come.

As the years rolled by, Keane continued to shape the footballing landscape with his unwavering dedication and sharp footballing mind. Despite stepping away from the spotlight as a player, his influence remained palpable.

In 2013, Keane returned to the international stage, this time as assistant manager of the Republic of Ireland national team, working alongside manager Martin O'Neill. His leadership and tactical acumen provided invaluable support to the team, as they navigated the highs and lows of international competition.

Keane's coaching journey also saw him take on brief assistant manager roles at Aston Villa and Nottingham Forest, where his wealth of experience and no-nonsense approach left an indelible mark on the players under his guidance.

Away from the sidelines, Keane's insights and analysis captivated audiences as he graced the screens of British channels ITV and Sky Sports, offering his unique perspective on the beautiful game.

Through it all, Keane remained a towering figure in the world of football, revered for his tenacity, leadership, and unyielding pursuit of excellence. His journey from the fields of Cork to the hallowed grounds of Old Trafford epitomized the power of passion and perseverance.

As the final whistle blew on his illustrious career, Roy Maurice Keane left an enduring legacy—one defined not only by trophies and accolades but by the unwavering commitment to giving his all, both on and off the pitch.

In the hearts of football fans around the world, the name Roy Keane will forever evoke memories of grit, determination, and the relentless pursuit of greatness—a true legend of the game.

With each passing chapter of his life, Roy Keane continued to redefine what it meant to be a footballing icon. Beyond the trophies and accolades, his story resonated with fans worldwide, transcending the boundaries of the pitch.

As he stepped into the role of pundit and analyst, Keane's sharp wit and uncompromising honesty brought a new dimension to football coverage. Whether dissecting tactics or critiquing performances, his words carried the weight of experience and a deep-rooted passion for the game.

Off the field, Keane's philanthropic efforts endeared him to communities far and wide. His commitment to charitable causes, from supporting youth development programs to championing mental health initiatives, showcased a compassionate side that often went unseen amidst the roar of the crowd.

Despite the passage of time, Keane's legacy remained etched in the annals of football history. His name became synonymous with courage, resilience, and the relentless pursuit of excellence—a testament to the enduring power of the human spirit.

As the sun set on his storied career, Roy Keane stood as a beacon of inspiration for future generations of footballers, coaches, and fans alike. His journey from humble beginnings to global acclaim served as a reminder that greatness is not merely achieved through talent, but through unwavering determination and an unyielding commitment to one's dreams.

And so, as the final whistle echoed across stadiums far and wide, one thing remained abundantly clear: Roy Maurice Keane had left an indelible mark on the beautiful game, forever cementing his place among the pantheon of footballing legends.

Roy Maurice Keane's story begins in the heart of Cork, Ireland, where he was born into a family where hard work and love for sports ran deep. Growing up in the Ballinderry Park area of Cork's Mayfield suburb, Roy's father, Maurice, epitomized the spirit of resilience, taking on various jobs to support his family, from the local knitwear company to the bustling Murphy's Irish Stout brewery.

Sports, particularly football, held a special place in the Keane household. It seemed a natural progression for young Roy, who was drawn to the beautiful game from an early age. His roots in football were nurtured by the tales of relatives who had donned the jerseys of junior Cork clubs like Rockmount. Yet, it wasn't just football that captured Roy's attention; he also found himself drawn to the ring, taking up boxing at the tender age of nine. With determination and skill, he quickly made a name for himself, winning all four of his bouts in the novice league.

But it was on the football pitch where Roy truly found his calling. Even in his early years at Rockmount, his talent shone brightly, earning him the title of "Player of the Year" in his very first season—a testament to his innate ability and relentless work ethic. While many of his teammates were offered trials with English football teams, Roy's path seemed less certain.

Despite the trials and tribulations, Roy's passion for the game burned brightly. As a child, he cheered on Celtic and Tottenham Hotspur, finding inspiration in the likes of Liam Brady and Glenn Hoddle. However, it was a Manchester United icon who would capture his admiration and shape his footballing dreams—Bryan Robson.

In these formative years, Roy Keane's journey was already taking shape, fueled by a determination to defy the odds and carve out his place in the annals of footballing history. Little did he know, his name would one day be synonymous with greatness, leaving an indelible mark on the sport he loved so dearly.

As Roy Maurice Keane matured, his passion for football intensified, fueled by the dreams of emulating his heroes and leaving a lasting legacy on the pitch. Despite the initial setbacks, his resolve only strengthened, driving him to pursue his footballing dreams with unwavering determination.

With each passing year, Roy honed his skills on the fields of Cork, relentlessly chasing his goal of making it big in the world of football. His commitment to the game was unwavering, spending countless hours practicing his craft, fine-tuning his technique, and honing his instincts on the pitch.

But it wasn't just talent that set Roy apart—it was his relentless work ethic, his refusal to back down from any challenge, and his unyielding determination to succeed against all odds. These qualities propelled him forward, earning him recognition as one of the most promising talents to emerge from the streets of Cork.

As he continued to excel on the football pitch, Roy's admiration for Bryan Robson evolved into a burning desire to follow in his footsteps, to wear the iconic red jersey of Manchester United and lead his team to glory.

Little did he know that his childhood dreams were on the brink of becoming a reality, as destiny prepared to weave the threads of his remarkable journey into the tapestry of footballing history.

Undeterred by early setbacks and the skepticism of others, Roy Maurice Keane's unwavering determination propelled him forward on his quest for footballing greatness. Rejected from the Ireland schoolboys squad and turned down by numerous English clubs, Keane refused to let adversity stand in the way of his dreams.

As the years passed, he juggled temporary jobs with his relentless pursuit of a breakthrough in football. It was in 1989 that fate intervened, leading him to sign for the semi-professional Irish club, Cobh Ramblers. Persuaded by the youth team manager, Eddie O'Rourke, Keane took his first steps into the world of senior football, seizing the opportunity to train full-time as part of the FAI/FAS scheme in Palmerstown.

Living in nearby Leixlip, County Kildare, from Monday to Friday, Keane immersed himself in the rigorous training regimen, determined to make the most of every opportunity. His rapid progression was evident as he juggled commitments between the youth team and the first team, often playing twice in a single weekend to showcase his talent.

Keane's debut for Cobh Ramblers came on a fateful day in Buckley Park, where despite a 2-0 defeat to Kilkenny City in the Opel League Cup, his potential shone brightly. It wasn't long before he made his mark in the League of Ireland, earning his first senior appearance against Bray Wanderers.

With each match, Keane's star continued to rise, drawing the attention of scouts from across the water. It was during an FAI Youth Cup match against Belvedere that his performance caught the eye of Nottingham Forest scout Noel McCabe. Impressing the legendary Brian Clough during his trial, Keane's talent could no longer be denied.

In the summer of 1990, a deal worth £47,000 was struck, marking the beginning of a new chapter in Roy Keane's remarkable journey. From the humble fields of Cork to the hallowed grounds of English football, his rise to prominence was only just beginning—a testament to his unyielding spirit and relentless pursuit of excellence.

With a mixture of excitement and determination, Roy Keane embarked on the next phase of his footballing odyssey. Leaving behind the familiar sights and sounds of Cork, he set his sights on Nottingham Forest, eager to prove himself on the grand stage of English football.

Joining the ranks of Nottingham Forest, a club steeped in tradition and history, was a dream come true for the young Irishman. Under the tutelage of the legendary Brian Clough, Keane found himself surrounded by seasoned professionals and experienced mentors, eager to guide him on his journey to greatness.

From the moment he stepped onto the training ground, Keane's intensity and drive set him apart. With each passing day, he honed his skills, soaking up knowledge like a sponge and pushing himself to new heights.

It wasn't long before Keane's talent caught the eye of fans and pundits alike. His commanding presence in midfield, coupled with his fierce determination and unwavering work ethic, made him an indispensable asset to the Forest side.

In the years that followed, Keane's star continued to rise, as he cemented his reputation as one of the brightest talents in English football. His performances on the pitch spoke volumes, earning him recognition and admiration from fans across the country.

With his time at Nottingham Forest leaving an indelible mark on his career, Roy Keane stood at the precipice of greatness, poised to take the next monumental step in his footballing journey.

The call from Manchester United, one of the most storied clubs in the world, came as both a validation of his talent and a daunting challenge. Yet, for Keane, it was an opportunity he couldn't pass up—a chance to test himself against the best, to write his name in the annals of footballing history alongside legends of the game.

Arriving at Old Trafford, Keane was greeted with the weight of expectations, but he embraced the challenge with characteristic determination and grit. Under the guidance of the iconic Sir Alex Ferguson, he quickly asserted himself as a linchpin in the United midfield, a force to be reckoned with on the pitch.

His debut for the Red Devils marked the beginning of a new era, as Keane's commanding presence and unwavering commitment propelled United to new heights. With each passing season, he etched his name into the fabric of the club, leading by example and inspiring his teammates to greatness.

Keane's tenure at Manchester United was defined by moments of sheer brilliance, from his heroic performances in the heat of battle to his iconic leadership as club captain. Under his guidance, United soared to unprecedented success, claiming seven Premier League titles, four FA Cups, and the coveted UEFA Champions League.

But it wasn't just the silverware that defined Keane's legacy—it was his unwavering passion, his fierce determination, and his unyielding will to win. Whether it was marshaling the midfield with surgical precision or lifting his teammates in times of adversity, he embodied the spirit of Manchester United, earning the adoration of fans around the world.

As he hung up his boots and bid farewell to Old Trafford, Keane left behind a legacy that would stand the test of time. From the fields of Cork to the grand stage of Manchester United, his journey was a testament to the power of perseverance, dedication, and the unwavering belief in oneself.

But his story was far from over, as new challenges and adventures awaited him on the horizon. Little did he know, his next chapter would see him don the green jersey of his beloved Ireland, leading his nation on a journey of hope, determination, and unbridled passion—a journey that would further cement his status as one of the greatest midfielders of his generation.

As Roy Keane's journey with Nottingham Forest unfolded, it was marked by both triumphs and challenges, shaping him into the formidable force that would later dominate the midfield at Manchester United.

Under the guidance of the legendary Brian Clough, Keane's talents blossomed on the pitch, as he quickly asserted himself as a key player in the Forest lineup. Despite the initial struggles of being away from his family, Keane found solace in Clough's understanding and support, grateful for the manager's generosity in granting him occasional trips home to Cork.

His early performances for Forest showcased his potential, with memorable moments like his winning penalty in a pre-season tournament and his first professional goal against Sheffield United solidifying his place in the team. Keane's rise to prominence was meteoric, as he became a regular starter, displacing established stars like Steve Hodge.

Yet, his time at Forest was not without its challenges. Despite his contributions, the club faced relegation, and Keane found himself courted by top Premier League clubs, including Blackburn Rovers. Negotiations for a move ensued, with Clough famously dubbing Keane a "greedy child" amidst contract disputes.

However, fate intervened in the eleventh hour, as a bureaucratic mishap scuttled Keane's move to Blackburn. In a twist of fate, Manchester United manager Alex Ferguson seized the opportunity, swooping in to secure Keane's signature for a then-British record transfer fee.

With the stroke of a pen, Keane's path diverged towards Old Trafford, setting the stage for the next chapter in his illustrious career. As he bid farewell to Nottingham Forest, he left behind a legacy of resilience, determination, and unwavering commitment—a legacy that would continue to shape the footballing landscape for years to come.

The turn of events that saw Roy Keane's move from Nottingham Forest to Manchester United was nothing short of serendipitous, altering the course of footballing history in a matter of days.

As negotiations between Keane and Blackburn Rovers reached an impasse, fate intervened in the form of a bureaucratic hiccup. With the paperwork for the transfer stalled over the weekend, an unexpected opportunity arose.

Manchester United's legendary manager, Sir Alex Ferguson, wasted no time in seizing the moment. Hearing of Keane's impending move, Ferguson reached out with an enticing proposition—one that would see Keane don the iconic red jersey of Manchester United.

In a whirlwind of events, Keane found himself faced with a monumental decision. With the promise of a new chapter at Old Trafford beckoning, he seized the opportunity with both hands, embracing the challenge that lay ahead.

In a historic move, Manchester United secured Keane's signature for a British transfer record fee of £3.75 million, laying the foundation for one of the most illustrious careers in footballing history.

Little did Keane know, his journey at Manchester United would be defined by moments of triumph, adversity, and unbridled passion—a journey that would see him etch his name into the annals of footballing folklore forever.

As Roy Keane donned the iconic red jersey of Manchester United, he faced the daunting task of proving himself worthy of the then-record transfer fee. With midfield stalwarts Paul Ince and Bryan Robson holding court, Keane's path to the first team seemed uncertain.

However, fate intervened as injuries sidelined Robson, paving the way for Keane to establish himself as a mainstay in the United lineup. He wasted no time in making his mark, announcing his arrival with a sensational home debut, netting twice in a 3-0 victory against Sheffield United.

But it was in the heat of the Manchester derby that Keane truly endeared himself to the United faithful, scoring the winner as the Red Devils overturned a 2-0 deficit to secure a memorable 3-2 victory over arch-rivals Manchester City.

Keane's meteoric rise continued as he played a pivotal role in United's historic double-winning campaign. From lifting the Premier League trophy to securing a resounding 4-0 victory over Chelsea in the FA Cup Final, Keane etched his name into the annals of footballing history, establishing himself as a force to be reckoned with on the grand stage.

Despite the highs of the double-winning season, Keane's journey was not without its challenges. The following season saw United fall short in both the league and FA Cup, with Keane enduring his fair share of setbacks, including a red card in the FA Cup semi-final replay against Crystal Palace.

Yet, amidst the trials and tribulations, Keane's indomitable spirit shone through. As the summer of 1995 brought about a period of change at United, Keane emerged as the bedrock of the midfield, guiding a new generation of talent to glory.

The 1995–96 campaign saw Keane lead United to another Premier League title, staging a remarkable comeback to overcome Newcastle United's commanding 12-point lead and secure the championship once again. His influence on the pitch was matched only by his determination to succeed, as he helped clinch the FA Cup for a record ninth time with a hard-fought 1–0 victory over Liverpool.

Yet, despite his stellar performances, Keane's journey was not without its share of adversity. Knee injuries and suspensions plagued the following season, casting doubt over his future at the club. However, true to form, Keane rose above the challenges, proving his mettle time and time again as he continued to lead United to glory on both domestic and European fronts.

With each passing season, Roy Keane's legacy at Manchester United grew, his name forever etched in the annals of footballing history as one of the greatest midfielders to ever grace the hallowed grounds of Old Trafford.

Amidst the highs and lows of his tenure at Manchester United, Roy Keane's unwavering commitment to excellence remained the driving force behind his remarkable journey.
Despite the setbacks of injuries and suspensions, Keane's leadership on and off the pitch continued to inspire his teammates to greatness. His ferocious determination and relentless work ethic set the standard for those around him, pushing United to new heights of success.

As the 1997–98 season dawned, Keane faced yet another test of character. With the weight of expectations resting heavily on his shoulders, he rose to the occasion once more, leading United to yet another Premier League title.

But it was in the crucible of European competition that Keane truly showcased his mettle. Despite a disappointing exit from the Champions League at the hands of Borussia Dortmund, his heroic performances and unwavering resolve endeared him to fans around the world.

As the curtain fell on his early years at Manchester United, Keane's legacy was already secure. From his electrifying debut to his championship-winning heroics, he had etched his name into the fabric of the club, forever cementing his status as a true legend of the game.
But little did he know, his greatest challenges and triumphs still lay ahead, as destiny prepared to beckon him towards a new chapter in his storied career—one that would see him don the armband of his beloved Ireland and lead his nation on a journey of hope, determination, and unbridled passion.

As Roy Keane assumed the mantle of club captain at Manchester United, he faced the immense challenge of filling the void left by the departure of Eric Cantona. However, his early tenure as captain was marred by a devastating cruciate ligament injury sustained in a clash with Leeds United's Alfie Haaland.

The incident, steeped in controversy and animosity, would cast a shadow over Keane's career for years to come. As he lay prone on the ground, Haaland's accusations and the subsequent fallout would ignite a fierce rivalry between the two players.

Keane's absence during the 1997–98 season was keenly felt by United, as they squandered an 11-point lead over Arsenal, missing out on the Premier League title. Pundits pointed to Keane's absence as a pivotal factor in the team's downfall, highlighting his indispensable presence both on and off the pitch.

However, Keane's return to the side the following season heralded a period of unprecedented success for Manchester United. Under his leadership, the Red Devils secured a historic treble, winning the FA Premier League, FA Cup, and UEFA Champions League in a single season.

In a moment of sheer brilliance against Juventus in the Champions League semi-final, Keane inspired his team to a remarkable comeback from two goals down, scoring the first United goal and epitomizing the spirit of determination and resilience that defined his career. Despite receiving a yellow card that ruled him out of the final, United emerged victorious over Bayern Munich, securing their place in footballing history.

Yet, amidst the triumphs, Keane's journey was not without its share of challenges and controversies. Contract negotiations with the club saw tensions rise, with Keane eventually securing a lucrative deal after prolonged negotiations. However, his candid criticism of certain sections of United supporters following a Champions League victory over Dynamo Kyiv sparked debate and controversy, highlighting the changing atmosphere in football grounds.

Despite the controversies, Keane's leadership and unwavering commitment to excellence continued to inspire those around him, cementing his legacy as one of the greatest captains in Manchester United's storied history. As he led the Red Devils to unparalleled success on both domestic and European fronts, his name became synonymous with courage, determination, and the relentless pursuit of victory.

The infamous incident involving Alfie Haaland and Roy Keane during the 2001 Manchester derby would go down in footballing history as one of the most controversial and contentious moments of Keane's career.

With just five minutes remaining in the match, Keane delivered a knee-high tackle on Haaland, an action that many viewed as an act of revenge for an incident between the two players years earlier. Keane's tackle sparked outrage and condemnation from fans and pundits alike, with many labeling it as a deliberate and malicious assault.

Keane's subsequent admission in his autobiography, where he openly stated his intent to "hurt" Haaland, only added fuel to the fire. His candid account of the incident sent shockwaves through the footballing world, leading to further punishment from the Football Association (FA).

In the wake of his admission, Keane was charged with bringing the game into disrepute, resulting in a five-match ban and a hefty fine. Despite facing widespread condemnation, Keane remained unrepentant, expressing no regrets about his actions and maintaining that Haaland had received his "just rewards."

The fallout from the incident was significant, with Haaland's career ultimately cut short by a long-standing injury to his left knee. While some speculated that Keane's tackle had contributed to Haaland's decline, others pointed to the complexities of Haaland's injury history.

Regardless of the debates and controversies that surrounded the incident, one thing remained clear—Keane's tackle on Haaland would forever be etched into the annals of footballing lore, a testament to the intensity and passion that defined his career on the pitch.

In the twilight years of his illustrious career at Manchester United, Roy Keane continued to epitomize the qualities of leadership, determination, and unyielding commitment that had defined his tenure as club captain.

The 2001–02 season proved to be a challenging one for United, as they finished trophyless for the first time in four years. Despite their domestic shortcomings, progress was made in Europe, with United reaching the semi-finals of the Champions League. However, their hopes of European glory were dashed after a heartbreaking defeat to Bayer Leverkusen.

In the aftermath of the defeat, Keane made headlines for his scathing criticism of some of his teammates, accusing them of losing sight of their hunger for success amidst their pursuit of wealth and luxury. His outspoken remarks sparked controversy and debate, underscoring his unwavering commitment to excellence on the pitch.

Yet, amidst the challenges and setbacks, Keane's resolve remained unshakeable. Following a series of injuries and suspensions, he underwent hip surgery, facing the prospect of a career-threatening condition. However, Keane's determination to overcome adversity saw him return to the pitch stronger than ever, leading United to another league title in May 2003.

Throughout the 2000s, Keane engaged in a fierce rivalry with Arsenal captain Patrick Vieira, epitomizing the intense competition between two of English football's most iconic clubs. Their heated exchanges on and off the pitch only served to underscore Keane's unyielding passion and competitive spirit.

As his tenure at Manchester United drew to a close, Keane's legacy was firmly cemented. With nine major honours to his name, including seven FA Cup final appearances, he stood as the most successful captain in the club's storied history. His impact on the English game was further recognized with his induction into the English Football Hall of Fame and inclusion in the prestigious FIFA 100 list.

Despite his combative style of play and record number of red cards, Roy Keane's contributions to Manchester United and the broader footballing world transcended statistics, leaving an indelible mark on the sport and ensuring his place among the pantheon of footballing legends.

Roy Keane's departure from Manchester United in November 2005 marked the end of an era and brought to a close his illustrious tenure at the club.

His exit, characterized by mutual consent, came amidst a period of protracted absence from the team due to an injury sustained in his final competitive game—a robust challenge from Luis García during a match against Liverpool. Tensions had been mounting between Keane and the United management and players since a preseason training camp in Portugal, where disagreements with Sir Alex Ferguson over the quality of the setup at the resort emerged.

The situation escalated further when Keane openly admitted during an MUTV phone-in that he would be willing to play elsewhere after the expiration of his contract. A subsequent appearance on MUTV, in which he criticized several teammates' performances, including Rio Ferdinand, further strained relations and led to his departure.

Despite the controversies surrounding his exit, Keane left behind a legacy of remarkable achievement and leadership at Manchester United. With 33 league goals and a total of 51 in all competitions, he had played a pivotal role in the club's success over his 12-and-a-half-year tenure.

Keane's departure was marked by a testimonial match at Old Trafford between United and Celtic, with the proceeds donated to his favorite charity, the Irish Guide Dogs for the Blind. The match, attended by a capacity crowd of 69,591, served as a fitting tribute to Keane's remarkable career and enduring impact on the club.

Roy Keane's move to Celtic in December 2005 marked a return to his roots, as he joined the team he had supported as a child. Despite initial reports suggesting a lucrative contract offer, Keane later revealed in his autobiography that he was paid significantly less than speculated.

His Celtic career kicked off in January 2006, but it began on a sour note as the team suffered a shocking defeat to Clyde in the Scottish Cup. Keane's trademark intensity was evident as he didn't shy away from criticizing some of his new teammates during the match. However, he quickly asserted his leadership on the field, scoring his only goal for Celtic in a league victory over Falkirk and leading the team to victory in his first Old Firm derby against Rangers.

Despite his relatively short tenure at Celtic, Keane's impact was profound. He played a crucial role in guiding the team to a double of the Scottish Premier League title and Scottish League Cup, adding another honor to his illustrious career.

However, Keane's time at Celtic was cut short when he announced his retirement from professional football on medical advice in June 2006, just six months after joining the club. His decision to hang up his boots prompted widespread praise from former colleagues and managers, cementing his status as one of the greatest players of his generation. As Sir Alex Ferguson aptly put it, Roy Keane's name would undoubtedly feature in discussions of the best footballers of all time.

Roy Keane's international career with the Republic of Ireland was marked by both remarkable performances on the field and frequent clashes with team management.

His journey began at the youth level, where he showcased his talent as a budding footballer. However, his discontent with the organization and preparation surrounding the Irish team became evident early on, leading to confrontations with the management.

Despite these issues, Keane was a key figure in the Republic of Ireland's senior squad, particularly during major tournaments. He played a pivotal role in the 1994 FIFA World Cup, where Ireland achieved notable success, including a famous victory over Italy. Despite his individual contributions, Keane remained unsatisfied with the team's performance, reflecting his relentless pursuit of excellence.

In subsequent years, Keane continued to lead by example on the field, contributing to Ireland's qualification for the 2002 World Cup under new manager Mick McCarthy. His match-winning performances were instrumental in securing crucial victories against formidable opponents, cementing his status as a talisman for the national team.

However, tensions between Keane and the Irish management persisted, culminating in a high-profile confrontation during the 2002 World Cup. Keane's dispute with manager Mick McCarthy over the team's training facilities led to his expulsion from the squad, a decision that divided opinion among fans and pundits alike.

Despite the controversy, Keane's impact on Irish football was undeniable. His dedication, skill, and unwavering commitment to excellence left an indelible mark on the national team, earning him admiration and respect from fans and peers alike.

The Saipan incident during the 2002 FIFA World Cup marked a significant chapter in Roy Keane's international career with the Republic of Ireland, sparking controversy and dividing opinions within the team and among fans.

Keane's dissatisfaction with the training facilities and preparation for the World Cup came to a head during the team's training camp in Saipan. His heated exchanges with coaching staff and his decision to temporarily leave the squad highlighted the underlying tensions within the Irish camp.

Upon his return to the training camp, Keane's candid interview with a sports journalist further fueled the discord, leading to a confrontation with manager Mick McCarthy in front of the entire squad. Keane's scathing remarks towards McCarthy ultimately resulted in his dismissal from the squad and his subsequent departure from the World Cup.

The aftermath of the Saipan incident saw Keane's absence deeply felt by the Irish team, who ultimately exited the tournament in the round of 16. The incident also left a lasting impact on Irish football, sparking debates and discussions about player-manager relationships and the role of professionalism in the sport.

Despite the controversy surrounding the incident, Keane's influence and contribution to Irish football cannot be denied. His passion, commitment, and unwavering dedication to excellence remain part of his legacy, both on and off the field.

Roy Keane's recall to the Republic of Ireland national team under new manager Brian Kerr marked a significant turn of events in his international career. Despite his previous controversies and disagreements with the team management, Keane's return was a testament to his enduring talent and influence on the pitch.

Keane's comeback for the national team against Romania in May 2004 signaled a fresh start, albeit without the captaincy he once held. Despite this, his presence brought a sense of stability and experience to the Irish squad, as they aimed to secure qualification for major tournaments.

However, despite Keane's efforts, Ireland fell short of qualifying for the 2006 FIFA World Cup. Following this disappointment, Keane made the decision to retire from international football, opting to focus on prolonging his club career.

Keane's return and subsequent retirement from the national team reflected his complex relationship with Irish football, characterized by highs and lows, controversy, and redemption. His contributions to the Irish team will be remembered as both impactful and divisive, leaving a lasting legacy in the annals of Irish football history.

Roy Keane's post-retirement involvement in football has been marked by continued outspokenness and controversy, particularly regarding his views on the Football Association of Ireland (FAI) and the state of Irish football.

Keane's criticisms of the FAI extended to what he perceived as biases in player selection based on media exposure and regional origin. He argued that players from certain regions, particularly Dublin and Leinster, were favored over others, potentially impacting the national team's performance.

Following Ireland's controversial defeat to France in the qualification playoffs for the 2010 FIFA World Cup, Keane once again made headlines with his scathing remarks. He criticized both the team's defensive performance and the FAI's handling of the aftermath, particularly in light of the Thierry Henry handball incident.

Keane's willingness to speak candidly on sensitive issues within Irish football has earned him both praise and criticism. While some view his outspoken nature as refreshing and necessary for addressing underlying problems, others perceive it as divisive and damaging to the sport's reputation.

Despite his controversial remarks, Keane's passion for the game and his desire to see improvements in Irish football remain evident. His post-retirement involvement continues to spark debate and reflection within the football community.

Despite the uncertainty surrounding his managerial prospects at Manchester United, Roy Keane pursued a career in coaching and management following his retirement as a player.

Keane's first managerial role came at Sunderland, where he was appointed manager in August 2006. He quickly made an impact, leading the club to promotion from the Football League Championship to the Premier League in his first season in charge. His tenure at Sunderland was marked by his no-nonsense approach and strong leadership, qualities that had defined his playing career.

After leaving Sunderland in December 2008, Keane went on to manage Ipswich Town from April 2009 to January 2011. His time at Ipswich was less successful than his spell at Sunderland, with the club failing to achieve promotion to the Premier League during his tenure.

Keane has also had coaching roles with the Republic of Ireland national team and has worked as an assistant manager at clubs including Aston Villa and Nottingham Forest.

While Keane's managerial career has had its ups and downs, his experience as a player and his strong personality have made him a respected figure in the world of football coaching. Despite the challenges he has faced, Keane remains passionate about the game and continues to contribute to the sport in various coaching capacities.

Roy Keane's tenure at Sunderland marked a significant chapter in both his managerial career and the club's history. Despite joining the club when they were struggling in the Championship, Keane's leadership and tactical acumen quickly transformed Sunderland's fortunes.

Under Keane's guidance, Sunderland achieved promotion to the Premier League in his first season, followed by clinching the Championship title. Keane's hands-on approach and strict disciplinary measures instilled a new sense of professionalism within the squad, leading to improved performances on the pitch.

However, Sunderland's Premier League journey under Keane faced challenges, including heavy defeats and inconsistent form. Despite some notable victories, Keane ultimately stepped down as manager in December 2008 amid growing pressure and reported tensions with key figures at the club.

Despite the ups and downs, Keane's impact on Sunderland was profound, laying the groundwork for future success and earning him recognition as the Championship Manager of the Year. His departure marked the end of a significant era for the club, but Keane's legacy continued to influence its trajectory in the years to come.

Roy Keane's tenure at Ipswich Town was marked by mixed results and ultimately ended in disappointment. Despite starting with a promising win over Cardiff City, the team struggled to find consistency under Keane's leadership.

Keane made several signings, including players from his former club Sunderland, in an attempt to strengthen the squad. However, Ipswich's poor form persisted, with the team failing to secure victories in their first 14 matches of the 2009-2010 season.

While there were some improvements in performance as the season progressed, Ipswich's inability to convert draws into wins saw them finish in a mid-table position. The following season saw similar inconsistencies, with the team struggling to challenge for promotion and even facing relegation concerns at times.

Ultimately, Keane's tenure at Ipswich Town came to an end in January 2011, following a period of poor results and mounting pressure. Despite his efforts, he was unable to achieve the desired success at the club, and his departure marked the conclusion of his time in charge.

Roy Keane's role as assistant manager of the Republic of Ireland national team was marked by both successes and controversies. Alongside manager Martin O'Neill, he helped lead the team to victories in important matches, including a 3-0 win against Latvia.

However, Keane's tenure was also marred by controversies, including incidents with fans and confrontations with journalists. His outspoken nature and tendency to make provocative comments sometimes overshadowed the team's performances.

Keane's involvement in incidents such as the confrontation with a fan in a team hotel and his comments about Everton putting pressure on Irish players added to the media scrutiny surrounding him. Despite support from the FAI and O'Neill, his actions sometimes drew criticism and raised questions about his role within the team.

Ultimately, Keane and O'Neill parted ways with the national team in November 2018, ending their tenure by mutual agreement.

Roy Keane joined Aston Villa as the assistant manager on July 1, 2014, under manager Paul Lambert. He juggled this position with his role as the assistant manager of the Republic of Ireland national team. However, Keane's stint at Aston Villa was short-lived, as he resigned from his position on November 28, 2014, to focus solely on his responsibilities with the Irish national team.

In January 2019, Roy Keane took on the role of assistant manager at Nottingham Forest. However, he left the position in June 2019, after a brief tenure with the club.

Roy Keane was renowned for his commanding presence in midfield, characterized by his relentless work ethic, physicality, and competitive nature. He possessed exceptional stamina, intelligence, and positional awareness, enabling him to excel in both defensive and attacking roles. Keane's tenacity, aggression, and ball-winning abilities made him a formidable opponent in midfield battles, while his composure on the ball, precise passing, and ability to dictate the tempo of the game showcased his technical prowess.

Throughout his career, Keane evolved from a dynamic box-to-box midfielder to a deeper-lying playmaker, adapting his style to compensate for his physical decline. Despite this shift, he remained influential on the pitch, displaying strong leadership qualities and a determined mentality. Keane's commitment to excellence set a high standard for his teammates, earning him respect and admiration as a leader.

Off the field, Keane's personality was described as complex, characterized by his intense competitiveness on the pitch juxtaposed with a shy, introverted demeanor in private. Despite his public persona, Keane's teammates and coaches recognized his unwavering dedication to success and his ability to inspire those around him to perform at their best.

Roy Keane had a decorated career both as a player and a manager, earning numerous honors and accolades:

As a player:

Nottingham Forest:

Full Members' Cup: 1991–92
Manchester United:

Premier League: 1993–94, 1995–96, 1996–97, 1998–99, 1999–2000, 2000–01, 2002–03
FA Cup: 1993–94, 1995–96, 1998–99, 2003–04
FA Community Shield: 1993, 1996, 1997, 2003
UEFA Champions League: 1998–99
Intercontinental Cup: 1999
Celtic:

Scottish Premier League: 2005–06
Scottish League Cup: 2005–06
Individual:

PFA Team of the Year: Multiple times
FAI Young International Player of the Year: 1993, 1994
FAI Senior International Player of the Year: 1997, 2001
Premier League Player of the Month: October 1998, December 1999
Sir Matt Busby Player of the Year: 1999, 2000
RTÉ Sports Person of the Year: 1999
FWA Footballer of the Year: 2000
PFA Players' Player of the Year: 2000
FIFA 100
Premier League Hall of Fame: 2021

As a manager:

Sunderland:

Football League Championship: 2006–07
Individual:

Football League Championship Manager of the Month: February 2007, March 2007
LMA Championship Manager of the Year: 2006–07
Orders and special awards:

Cork Person of the Year: 2004
Honorary Doctorate of Law: 2002
Keane's illustrious career is a testament to his talent, dedication, and impact on the football world as both a player and a manager.

Roy Keane has had a varied media career, initially expressing reluctance but eventually becoming a prominent figure in football punditry. Here's a summary:

Initially, Keane expressed a lack of enthusiasm for media work, stating his aversion to appearing as a pundit, particularly criticizing the commentary style and the atmosphere surrounding television coverage.

However, he later had a change of heart and began working as a pundit for ITV's coverage of football matches, including the Champions League final and FA Cup matches.

In the 2011-12 season, Keane became ITV's chief football analyst, appearing regularly alongside presenters Adrian Chiles and Gareth Southgate, covering a wide range of matches including the Champions League, FA Cup, and England internationals.

During his time as assistant manager for the Republic of Ireland, Keane also contributed to UEFA Champions League and UEFA Europa League highlights shows on ITV between 2015 and 2018.

Keane continued to work for ITV during major tournaments such as the FIFA World Cup and UEFA European Championship, providing analysis and commentary on matches.

In 2019, Keane joined Sky Sports to work on their Super Sunday coverage, further expanding his presence in football media.

Despite his initial reservations, Keane has become a well-known and respected figure in football punditry, offering his insights and opinions on various aspects of the game.

Roy Keane's personal life includes his marriage to Theresa Doyle in 1997, with whom he has five children. Over the years, they have lived in various homes, including a modern house in Bowdon and a mock Tudor mansion in Hale during his time at Manchester United. Later, they had a new house built near Hale, valued at £2.5 million. In 2009, they purchased a house in the Ipswich area, closer to the training ground of Keane's club, Ipswich Town, where they settled in the market town of Woodbridge.

In addition to his football career, Keane has also authored autobiographies. The second part of his autobiography, titled "The Second Half," was released in October 2014. It was ghostwritten by Roddy Doyle and serves as a follow-up to his first autobiography, which was released in 2002 and ghostwritten by Eamon Dunphy.

Triggs, Roy Keane's beloved Labrador Retriever, was more than just a pet; she was a constant companion through the highs and lows of his life and career. Triggs gained international attention during the Saipan incident in 2002, where Keane famously remarked, "Unlike humans, dogs don't talk shit." Triggs became a symbol of loyalty and companionship, accompanying Keane on long walks and offering him solace during difficult times.

Triggs's fame extended beyond football circles, with media outlets often referencing her in connection with Keane's activities. Her presence brought light-heartedness to press coverage, with reporters joking about her fitness and endurance. Triggs was even involved in a police investigation at one point, highlighting her significance in Keane's life.

In 2009, Triggs appeared in an advertisement for the Irish Guide Dogs for the Blind, solidifying her status as a celebrity canine. Erroneous reports of her death in 2010 prompted an outpouring of sympathy, underscoring the deep bond between Keane and his faithful companion. Triggs's legacy lives on as a symbol of loyalty, steadfastness, and unwavering support in the life of one of football's most iconic figures.

It's fascinating how real-life personalities can inspire fictional characters. Roy Kent, the gruff and no-nonsense footballer portrayed in the TV series Ted Lasso, draws inspiration from Roy Keane's demeanor and reputation. While there may be some similarities between the two, Keane himself humorously insists that he's "a lot nicer" than his on-screen counterpart. It's a testament to Keane's impact on the world of football that his persona continues to resonate in popular culture, even in fictionalized form.

Printed in Great Britain
by Amazon